MANAGEMENT DEVELOPMENT SUPER SERIES

THIRD EDITION

Managing People

Becoming More Effective

Published for
&NEBS Management by Pergamon Flexible Learning

Pergamon Flexible Learning
An imprint of Butterworth-Heinemann
Linacre House, Jordan Hill, Oxford OX2 8DP
225 Wildwood Avenue, Woburn, MA 01801-2041
A division of Reed Educational and Professional Publishing Ltd

A member of the Reed Elsevier plc group

OXFORD   AUCKLAND   BOSTON
JOHANNESBURG   MELBOURNE   NEW DELHI

First published 1986
Second edition 1991
Third edition 1997
Reprinted 1998, 1999, 2000, 2002

© NEBS Management 1986, 1991, 1997

All rights reserved. No part of this publication may be reproduced in any material form (including photocopying or storing in any medium by electronic means and whether or not transiently or incidentally to some other use of this publication) without the written permission of the copyright holder except in accordance with the provisions of the Copyright, Designs and Patents Act 1988 or under the terms of a licence issued by the Copyright Licensing Agency Ltd, 90 Tottenham Court Road, London, England W1P 0LP. Applications for the copyright holder's written permission to reproduce any part of this publication should be addressed to the publishers

British Library Cataloguing in Publication Data
A catalogue record for this book is available from the British Library

ISBN 0 7506 3322 0

For more information on all Butterworth-Heinemann publications please visit our website at www.bh.com

The views expressed in this work are those of the authors and do not necessarily reflect those of the National Examining Board for Supervision and Management or of the publisher.

NEBS Management Project Manager: Diana Thomas
Author: Paul Shanahan
Editor: Diana Thomas
Series Editor: Diana Thomas
Composition by Genesis Typesetting, Rochester, Kent
Printed and bound in Great Britain

PLANT A TREE
British Trust for Conservation Volunteers
FOR EVERY TITLE THAT WE PUBLISH, BUTTERWORTH-HEINEMANN
WILL PAY FOR BTCV TO PLANT AND CARE FOR A TREE.

Contents

Workbook introduction v
1. NEBS Management Super Series 3 study links v
2. S/NVQ links vi
3. Workbook objectives vi
4. Activity planner vii

Session A Assessing your effectiveness 1
1. Introduction 1
2. How effective are you? 2
3. What is stopping you being more effective? 6
4. Thinking about the kind of person you are 7
5. Self-management and personal development 8
6. **Summary** 13

Session B Improving your thinking and feeling 15
1. Introduction 15
2. Improving your thinking 15
3. Working with your feelings 23
4. **Summary** 29

Session C Personal drive and personal development 31
1. Introduction 31
2. Harnessing your personal drive 31
3. Changing yourself 38
4. Where do you go from here? 44
5. **Summary** 47

Performance checks 49
1. Quick quiz 49
2. Workbook assessment 51
3. Work-based assignment 52

Reflect and review 55
1. Reflect and review 55
2. Action plan 57
3. Extensions 59
4. Answers to self-assessment questions 60
5. Answers to the quick quiz 62
6. Certificate 64

Workbook introduction

1 NEBS Management Super Series 3 study links

Here are the workbook titles in each module which link with *Becoming More Effective*, should you wish to extend your study to other Super Series workbooks. There is a brief description of each workbook in the User Guide.

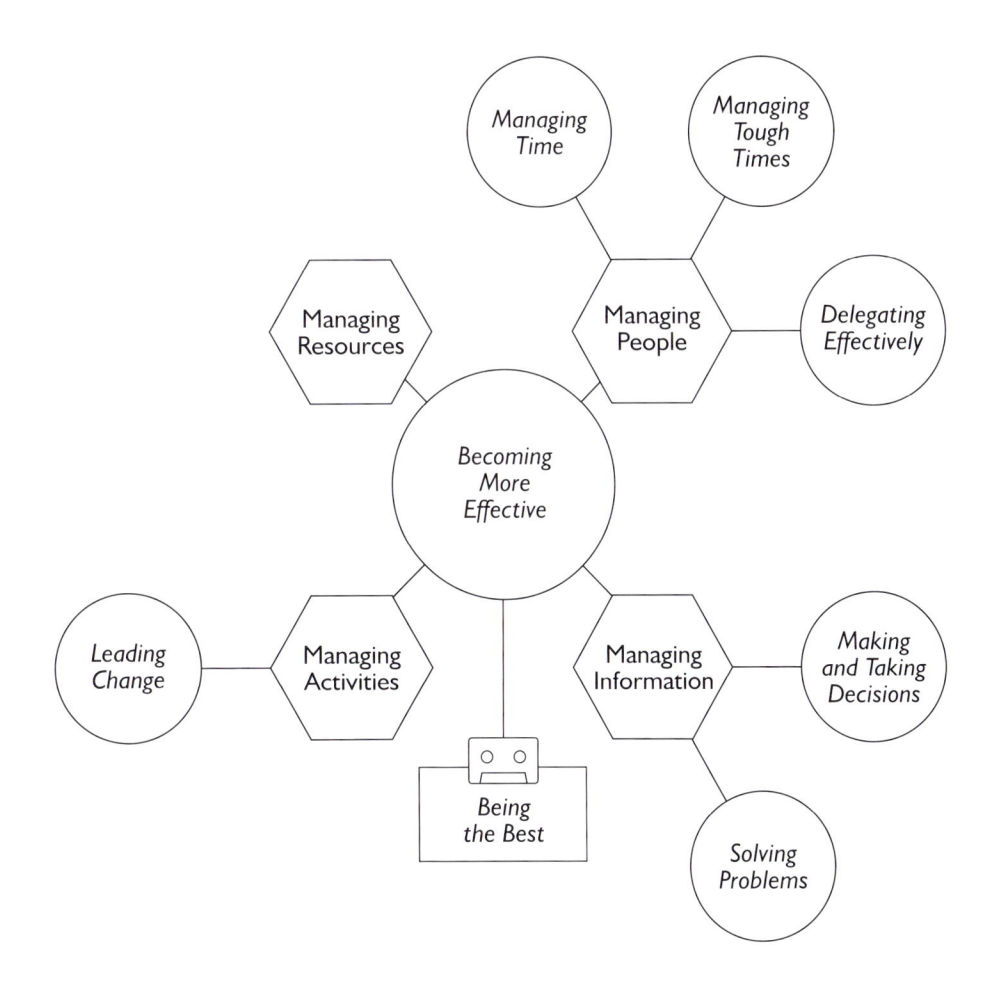

Workbook introduction

2 S/NVQ links

This workbook relates to the following elements:

C.1.1 Develop your own skills to improve your performance
C.1.2 Manage your time to meet your objectives

It will also help you to develop the following Personal Competences:

- acting assertively;
- behaving ethically;
- developing self confidence and personal drive;
- managing personal learning and development;
- acting strategically.

3 Workbook objectives

Every workbook in NEBS Super Series 3 is designed to make you more effective. So why is there a workbook specifically called 'Becoming More Effective'? In all the other workbooks in this series the emphasis is upon you acquiring knowledge and skills that will help you be more effective in managing resources, money, quality, other people, information, and so on. In this workbook the emphasis is on **you** as the person who has to acquire this knowledge and these skills and then put them to good use in your place of work. How well you can do this depends on how good you are as a self-manager.

In this workbook you will look at how well you can manage yourself. You will consider your strengths and weaknesses as a self-manager. This requires you to have a clear picture of yourself, to be able to think about yourself as if you were thinking about somebody else. You need to understand your feelings, to be able to master and use them as tools in your working life, rather than being their servant or even their slave. You need to be clear about what your aims or goals at work and in life generally are, since these are what energize you and enable you to translate what you can potentially do into what you actually do. You need to be able to evaluate what you do for its effectiveness and for its ethical consequences. Lastly, you need to be able to learn and, even more fundamentally, change yourself so that your weaknesses can become strengths and your strengths become still stronger. In today's rapidly moving world, staying the same is no longer an option.

3.1 Objectives

When you have completed this workbook you will be better able to:

- understand what self-management is all about;
- assess how well you manage yourself;
- see how your thinking can become more penetrating and creative;
- recognize that feelings are an essential part of working life and that they can be assets not liabilities;
- work on your personal drive;
- manage your learning and personal change to develop the capabilities you will need to stay effective.

4 Activity planner

The following activities require some planning so you may want to look at these now:

- Activity 2 on page 3 which asks you to review your areas of knowledge and skill in relation to your work;
- Activity 3 on page 6 which asks you to identify obstacles to your effectiveness;
- Activity 6 on page 10 which asks you to review your self-management;
- Activity 22 on page 36 which asks you to review ethical issues in your work;
- Activity 27 on page 45 which asks you to plan how you will improve your effectiveness.

Portfolio of evidence

Some or all of these Activities may provide the basis of evidence for your S/NVQ portfolio. All Portfolio Activities and the Work-based assignment are signposted with this icon.

The icon states the elements to which the Portfolio Activities and Work-based assignment relate.

The Work-based assignment (on page 52) suggests that you use a recent experience at work as an explicit learning opportunity. You might like to start thinking now about an experience from which you feel you could learn something significant.

Session A Assessing your effectiveness

1 Introduction

Being efficient is doing things right. Being effective is doing the right things. In this first session you have the opportunity to look at how effective you are and what might be stopping you being more effective. There are probably many obstacles preventing you being as effective as you would like. Some of these obstacles will be to do with things other than yourself. But some of the obstacles are likely to be connected with you: the kind of person you are, what you know and do not know, what you can and cannot do, how good you are at managing yourself as your most important resource and the one most under your control.

This session helps you diagnose those areas in your self-management which offer the greatest gains in improving your effectiveness. Later sessions will enable you to explore these areas more closely so that you can identify the actions that you can best take to become more effective.

Session A

2 How effective are you?

We'll start with an appraisal of just how effective you are at the moment.

Activity 1   2 mins

- Graham has been a team leader in a distribution warehouse for nine months. He had worked in the warehouse for seven years before being promoted and has excellent first hand knowledge of the business. But now that he has to achieve results through guiding and motivating the members of his team rather than doing things directly himself, he is finding his new job difficult. He is suddenly experiencing a lot of limitations in himself that he had previously been unaware of.

Do you think Graham's difficulties will reduce his overall level of effectiveness? Have you had similar experiences when you took on a new job?

No. His insight into what is needed and 'Running the job' should help him to support others in their work. His management of people may need development.

The job of a first line manager typically requires attention to many areas as well as the activities of the work: people, equipment, workspace, finance, quality, and so on. Not even the most competent manager is equally competent in all areas of their work. You probably find you are more 'at home' in certain parts of your job than others. Like Graham in the example, you may, for example, feel highly competent in the 'technical aspects' of your work, but extremely uncertain when dealing with people. But it is in facing up to your difficulties in those areas where you are uncomfortable that you can probably raise your overall level of effectiveness.

The Super Series 3 workbooks cover all the areas of work typically dealt with by first line managers. In Questionnaire 1 we have used all these workbook titles as a checklist for you to use in assessing your areas of effectiveness. In assessing your effectiveness in each area you might like to use a definition of effective as 'having an intended or expected effect' (*American Heritage Dictionary*).

Session A

Portfolio of evidence C1.1

Activity 2

15 mins

This Activity, together with Activities 3 and 6 later in this session, provide the foundations of evidence for your S/NVQ portfolio. You will return to these activities in Activity 27 in Session C, where you will have the opportunity to build on the results to provide evidence for your portfolio.

Look at Questionnaire 1 on pages 4 and 5. For each checklist item ask yourself to what extent you usually achieve either the effects you intended or the effects others (your manager, staff, customers, etc.) expect from you. Give yourself a rating from 1 to 5 where 1 equals very poor and 5 equals very good by circling the appropriate number in the middle column. For the moment do not put anything in the right-hand column. Be as honest as you can; the results of this questionnaire are for your benefit only, although you might like to check your ratings of yourself with somebody else who knows your work and who you can talk to freely.

Now work out your average rating for each of the four areas:

- Add up your Managing Activities ratings and divide by 9
- Add up your Managing Resources ratings and divide by 6
- Add up your Managing People ratings and divide by 15
- Add up your Managing Information ratings and divide by 10

Put your four averages in the table below:

Managing Activities: 3.5	Managing Resources: 3.3
Managing People: 3.6	Managing Information: 3.6

Doing this Activity should have helped you diagnose the areas where you are already effective and those areas where you would like to be more effective. But for those areas where you would like to be more effective you now need to look at **why** you are not more effective than you are.

Session A

Questionnaire 1. Assessing your effectiveness (see Activities 2 and 3)

NEBS Management Super Series 3 Workbooks	How effective are you?	What is stopping you being more effective?
A. Managing Activities		
1. Planning and Controlling Work	1 ----- 2 ---(3)--- 4 ----- 5	Time, pressure + demands
2. Understanding Quality	1 ----- 2 ----- 3 ---(4)--- 5	
3. Achieving Quality	1 ----- 2 ---(3)--- 4 ----- 5	Feeling I could have done more.
4. Caring for the Customer	1 ----- 2 ----- 3 ----- 4 ---(5)	
5. Marketing and Selling	1 ----- 2 ---(3)--- 4 ----- 5	Not always sure of best way to do it effectively.
6. Managing a Safe Environment	1 ----- 2 ----- 3 ---(4)--- 5	
7. Managing Lawfully – Health, Safety and Environment	1 ----- 2 ---(3)--- 4 ----- 5	Don't always invest as much time as I ought due to other work pressures.
8. Preventing Accidents	1 ----- 2 ----- 3 ---(4)--- 5	
9. Leading Change	1 ----- 2 ---(3)--- 4 ----- 5	Confidence
B. Managing Resources		
1. Controlling Physical Resources	1 ----- 2 ----- 3 ---(4)--- 5	
2. Improving Efficiency	1 ----- 2 ---(3)--- 4 ----- 5	Not always sure what would be the more efficient way.
3. Understanding Finance	1 ----- 2 ---(3)--- 4 ----- 5	Need for awareness about overall planning.
4. Working with Budgets	1 ----- 2 ----- 3 ---(4)--- 5	
5. Controlling Costs	1 ----- 2 ---(3)--- 4 ----- 5	Need for tighter monitoring.
6. Making a Financial Case	1 ----- 2 ---(3)--- 4 ----- 5	Unclear about best way to put proposal in.
C. Managing People		
1. How Organizations Work	1 ----- 2 ----- 3 ---(4)--- 5	
2. Managing with Authority	1 ----- 2 ---(3)--- 4 ----- 5	Confidence - not always having courage of convictions.
3. Leading Your Team	1 ----- 2 ---(3)--- 4 ----- 5	Sometimes a bit uncertain.
4. Delegating Effectively	1 ----- 2 ---(3)--- 4 ----- 5	Confidence about task completion.

Session A

NEBS Management Super Series 3 Workbooks	How effective are you?	What is stopping you being more effective?
5. Working in Teams	1 ----- 2 ----- 3 ----- 4 ----(5)	
6. Motivating People	1 ----- 2 ----- 3 ----(4)---- 5	
7. Securing the Right People	1 ----- 2 ----(3)---- 4 ----- 5	How to work with what we already have.
8. Appraising Performance	1 ----- 2 ----- 3 ----(4)---- 5	
9. Planning Training and Development	1 ----- 2 ----(3)---- 4 ----- 5	Influenced by outside factors often out of my control.
10. Delivering Training	1 ----- 2 ----- 3 ----(4)---- 5	
11. Managing Lawfully – People and Employment	1 ----- 2 ----(3)---- 4 ----- 5	Lack of knowledge in legal matters of employment law
12. Commitment to Equality	1 ----- 2 ----- 3 ----- 4 ----(5)	
13. *This workbook*	1 ----- 2 ----- 3 ----(4)---- 5	
14. Managing Tough Times	1 ----- 2 ----(3)---- 4 ----- 5	Rising to and dealing effectively with challenging colleagues.
15. Managing Time	1 ----- 2 ----(3)---- 4 ----- 5	Too emersed in dealing reactively.
D. Managing Information		
1. Collecting Information	1 ----- 2 ----- 3 ----(4)---- 5	
2. Storing and Retrieving Information	1 ----- 2 ----(3)---- 4 ----- 5	Personal organisation and confidence it will work. Trust or delegation.
3. Information in Management	1 ----- 2 ----- 3 ----(4)---- 5	
4. Communication in Management	1 ----- 2 ----- 3 ----(4)---- 5	
5. Listening and Speaking	1 ----- 2 ----- 3 ----(4)---- 5	
6. Communicating in Groups	1 ----- 2 ----- 3 ----(4)---- 5	
7. Writing Effectively	1 ----- 2 ----- 3 ----(4)---- 5	
8. Project and Report Writing	1 ----- 2 ----(3)---- 4 ----- 5	Dislike of paperwork.
9. Making and Taking Decisions	1 ----- 2 ----(3)---- 4 ----- 5	Not always sure about wider consequences & don't always take the long view
10. Solving Problems	1 ----- 2 ----(3)---- 4 ----- 5	Inability to always see the wider perspective

Session A

3 What is stopping you being more effective?

There are many obstacles to effectiveness. Now you can think about the ones that are affecting you.

Portfolio of evidence C1.1, C1.2

Activity 3

5 mins

This Activity may provide the basis of portfolio evidence which you will be able to develop further in Activity 27 in Session C.

Go back to Questionnaire 1. Now you can fill in the right-hand column headed 'What is stopping you being more effective?' For each topic in the checklist where you have rated your effectiveness as Fair, Poor or Very Poor (1, 2 or 3), write down one or more reasons why you are not more effective. (If you have rated yourself as Good or Very Good (4 or 5) on every topic, you are to be congratulated, but I also politely suggest you have another look at your ratings, perhaps with the help of a friendly but honest colleague.)

You may have written down all sorts of things which you experience as obstacles stopping you being more effective. Some of the more common obstacles are listed below:

- Lack of time/opportunity to acquire new knowledge and skills
- Lack of time/opportunity to practise skills
- Lack of guidance or support from managers
- Lack of support from staff
- Lack of technical or human resources
- Lack of time
- Lack of information/poor communications

All these are examples of what can be called 'outer obstacles'. They all originate in somebody or something other than you: somebody else is not telling you what you need to know; higher management is not giving you the staff or resources you need; your job does not give you time to keep up to date with new developments; and so on. These are all valid reasons and you may be able to do something about removing some of these obstacles. But there is often a deeper layer of what can be called 'inner obstacles'. These are obstacles that arise from the kind of person you are. To give a few examples: you may avoid new technology because you have fears that you cannot master it; new business methods may require a kind of thinking that is not how you are used to thinking; you may alienate your team through becoming angry too quickly; you may be unwilling to learn some new subject because you have lost interest in your work.

Activity 4

5 mins

- Mary is a supervisor in an insurance company. Over the past year her department has developed and implemented a new quality system. Mary's reaction to this has been that the new system is a lot of bureaucratic nonsense imposed by senior management. She feels that some of the freedom that she used to have in how she runs her team has been taken away. She has not openly raised the subject with her manager but is 'dragging her heels' over complying with the new system. Although in most respects Mary is extremely competent at her job, her resistance to the quality system is interfering with the work of her team and is causing difficulties with the other sections that rely on the work of her team.

Would you say that Mary's lack of effectiveness was due to an outer or an inner obstacle?

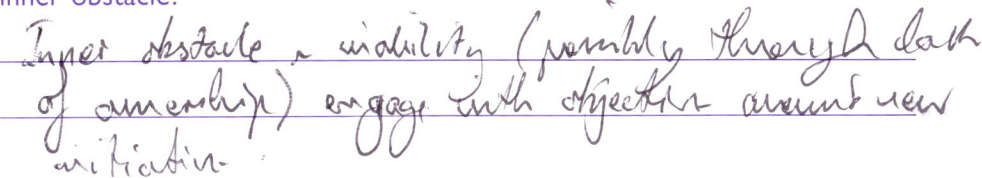

Inner obstacle - inability (possibly through lack of ownership) engage with objectives around new initiative.

Although the quality system is an 'outer event' imposed on Mary by others, I think that the main obstacle is an inner one: Mary's resistance. Since it is unrealistic to expect the unwanted quality system to disappear, if Mary wants to increase her effectiveness she must look at how she manages herself, in particular how she thinks and feels about the quality system. To do this Mary may have to confront her unwillingness to change herself.

4 Thinking about the kind of person you are

Inner obstacles usually have their roots in how we think about ourselves.

Activity 5

3 mins

Make a list of three or four things about yourself that you think may be inner obstacles to your effectiveness in some areas of your work. Begin your description of each obstacle with 'I'.

① I'm sometimes intimidated by strong personalities.
② I sometimes lack the confidence of my convictions.
③ I approach things sometimes at an emotional level rather than objectively.

Session A

Some of the kinds of inner obstacle you may have thought of are:

- I am simply no good with figures/technology/men/women/giving presentations . . .
- I am simply not a team player/salesperson/leader . . .
- I simply cannot stand engineers/arguments/working late . . .
- I simply don't think like accountants/lawyers/customers . . .
- I am simply not interested in computers/health and safety/other people's problems . . .
- I simply can't cope with change/senior managers/machines/bullies . . .

We often use the words 'simply' or 'just' in statements like these to say 'That is simply/just the way I am and there is nothing more to be done'. This may reflect a genuine belief that nothing can be done ('I have always been like this', 'I was born/made this way'), but such statements can also be used to hide an unwillingness to make the effort to change oneself. To increase one's personal effectiveness usually means accepting that we can change even very deep-seated personal characteristics, and accepting the responsibility that only we can change ourselves – nobody else can change the way we are.

5 Self-management and personal development

Self-management is about your ability to use your own personal resources in order to do your job effectively. Personal development is about enhancing your personal resources. What is meant by personal resources? Three of your most important personal resources are what are usually described as the three mental faculties:

- Thinking: Your ability to think clearly and creatively.
- Feeling: Your ability to relate to your work and the people around you through your emotions.
- Willing: Your ability to motivate yourself to take action. As a word 'willing' has a slightly old-fashioned sound, so although we use this word some of the time, we sometimes use a more modern equivalent, 'personal drive'.

There is in addition a fourth core personal faculty: your ability to change yourself. The ways you think, feel and will are not fixed forever. Through the effort of working on yourself you can change your thinking, feeling and willing. It is change at this deep level that is meant here by personal development.

what has been talked about so far. To be
 you usually need to be able to manage
ople and information (as reflected in the
 manage these areas you need knowledge
 simply **possessing** knowledge and skills is
le to put your knowledge and skills **into**
 Many people possess knowledge and skills
o their full effect. Putting knowledge and
ective self-management, which is the area
ure. Self-management means being able to
 and willing. At the very core of self-
ment, the ability to change the ways you
lf at work.

To manage activities, resources, people and information you need knowledge and skills. How well you can use your knowledge and skills depends on your self-management. Self-management involves the effective use of your thinking, feeling and willing. At the heart of self-management lies personal development which has the aim of increasing your ability to manage yourself.

Session A

Activity 6

Portfolio of evidence C1.1

15 mins

This Activity may form the basis of appropriate evidence for your S/NVQ portfolio. You will return to this in Activity 27 in Session C.

Questionnaire 2 is designed to help you assess your abilities in thinking, feeling, willing and personal development. You complete this questionnaire as follows. The questionnaire is made up of twenty pairs of statements. The statements in each pair are opposites of each other. Consider which of each pair is most true of you and use the scale 1 to 5 to indicate which statement best describes you. For example, the pair of statements in No. 6 are 'My personal feelings often get in the way of my work' and 'My personal feelings never get in the way of my work'. If you decide the first of these statements best describes you, then put a circle around number 1. If you feel that this statement almost but not quite describes you (your personal feelings **sometimes** get in the way of your work), then circle number 2. If you cannot decide which of the two statements best describes you, then circle number 3. Of course, if the second statement better describes you, then circle 4 or 5 depending on whether it is partly or totally accurate about you. Once again, the results of this questionnaire are only for your benefit, so try to be as honest with yourself as you can.

When you have rated yourself against all twenty statements, complete the following table. Look at your overall ratings for your thinking, feeling, willing and personal development to see which are your strongest and weakest areas.

THINKING:	FEELING:
Add up your ratings for statements 1 to 5 to find your overall rating of your thinking _18_	Add up your ratings for statements 6 to 10 to find your overall rating of your feeling _16_
WILLING:	PERSONAL DEVELOPMENT:
Add up your ratings for statements 11 to 15 to find your overall rating of your willing _19_	Add up your ratings for statements 16 to 20 to find your overall rating of your personal development _17_

Most people are not equally competent in all these four core personal faculties. Some people are very good at thinking, but poor at translating their ideas into action. Some people are strongly in touch with their feelings, but chaotic in their thinking. Some people rush into action, but before they have thought things through or worked out what they actually feel about what they

Session A

Questionnaire 2. Assessing your inner obstacles to effectiveness

1. I often fail to notice what is going on around me	1 ----- 2 ----- 3 -----(4)----- 5	I usually notice what is going on around me
2. I have trouble concentrating on one thing for any time	1 ----- 2 -----(3)----- 4 ----- 5	My powers of concentration are very strong
3. I am not good at following a logical argument	1 ----- 2 ----- 3 -----(4)----- 5	I am good at following a logical argument
4. I often cannot keep a good overview of what really matters	1 ----- 2 -----(3)----- 4 ----- 5	I can usually keep a good overview of what really matters
5. When asked for suggestions, I usually have no ideas to offer	1 ----- 2 ----- 3 -----(4)----- 5	When asked for suggestions, I usually have lots of good ideas
6. My personal feelings often get in the way of my work	1 -----(2)----- 3 ----- 4 ----- 5	My personal feelings never get in the way of my work
7. I never express my feelings at work	1 ----- 2 -----(3)----- 4 ----- 5	I find it can sometimes be helpful to express my feelings at work
8. I do not trust myself to cope in many working situations	1 ----- 2 ----- 3 -----(4)----- 5	I trust myself to cope in most working situations
9. I do not worry about being fair in dealing with others at work	1 ----- 2 ----- 3 -----(4)----- 5	I try to be fair in dealing with others at work
10. I am unclear about my personal values at work	1 ----- 2 -----(3)----- 4 ----- 5	I am clear about my personal values at work
11. In many working situations I am uncertain what I want	1 ----- 2 ----- 3 -----(4)----- 5	I usually know what I want in any working situation
12. I never think about the ethics of what I do at work	1 ----- 2 ----- 3 -----(4)----- 5	I often think about the ethics of what I do at work
13. I usually give in to pressure from others	1 ----- 2 -----(3)----- 4 ----- 5	I can usually resist pressure from others
14. I try to pass responsibility for my actions to others	1 ----- 2 ----- 3 -----(4)----- 5	I take full responsibility for my own actions
15. I have little energy or enthusiasm for my work	1 ----- 2 ----- 3 -----(4)----- 5	I approach my work full of energy and enthusiasm
16. I always assume I do a good job and have little room for improvement	1 ----- 2 ----- 3 -----(4)----- 5	I usually try to assess what I do at work to see where I can improve
17. I usually get angry or reject any suggestions that I need to change	1 ----- 2 -----(3)----- 4 ----- 5	I can usually listen calmly to any suggestions that I need to change
18. I take each day as it comes and hope I can cope with whatever arises	1 ----- 2 -----(3)----- 4 ----- 5	I am always looking ahead to prepare myself for future changes
19. I am poor at learning new things	1 ----- 2 -----(3)----- 4 ----- 5	I am good at learning new things
20. I never think about my own personal development	1 ----- 2 ----- 3 -----(4)----- 5	My own personal development is important to me

11

Session A

are doing. Some people may have reached a good level of competence in thinking, feeling and willing, but are stuck, unable to go any further through personal development. In the following sessions of this workbook, you will look first in more detail at how you can improve your effectiveness through working on your thinking, feeling and willing. Then you will look at how you can continue to improve in effectiveness, through making personal development an on-going part of your working life.

Self-assessment 1

10 mins

For questions 1 to 6 complete the sentences with a suitable word or words from the following list:

PERSONAL DEVELOPMENT	THINKING	INNER
PEOPLE	OUTER	INFORMATION
EFFECTIVE	RESOURCES	WILLING
EFFICIENT	SKILLS	FEELING

1 Being ___efficient___ is doing things right, being ___effective___ is doing the right things.

2 A manager needs to be effective at managing activities, ___resources___, ___information___ and ___people___.

3 Having the right knowledge and ___skills___ is necessary but not sufficient for being effective.

4 Obstacles to effectiveness can be ___outer___ or ___inner___.

5 ___Thinking___, ___feeling___ and ___willing___ are core personal skills.

6 ___Personal development___ is the process of improving your ability to manage yourself.

7 Give three examples of common outer obstacles to effectiveness:
   ___Unwillingness of others.___
   ___Conflicting priorities___
   ___Time.___

8 Who is the key person in improving your personal effectiveness?
   ___Yourself___

Answers to these questions can be found on page 60.

Session A

5 Summary

- Being efficient is doing things right, being effective is doing the right things.

- A manager usually manages activities, resources, people and information.

- Most people are not equally effective in all areas of their work.

- Managing activities, resources, people and information requires knowledge and skills.

- Knowledge and skills are not by themselves enough to be fully effective.

- Effectiveness at work needs effective self-management in order to make proper use of knowledge and skills.

- Self-management involves managing thinking, feeling and willing.

- Personal development is the process of improving one's self-management.

Session B Improving your thinking and feeling

1 Introduction

In Session A you saw that your core mental faculties are thinking, feeling, willing and personal development. These can be considered as abilities which lie at a deeper level than your technical, financial, people-management, and other more 'visible' skills. How you think about your work, how you feel about it, and what you want to bring about at work, are all central to your personal effectiveness. Personal development is about improving these faculties.

In this session you will look at the first two of these faculties, thinking and feeling, and see how you can improve. You may think that how you think and feel is too deeply rooted in your personal nature for you to change. But there is plenty of evidence that people can work on even these fundamental faculties to make themselves more effective. Certainly learning at this deep level can be difficult and takes time – far more than, say, learning a new word processing package. But it can be done – if you judge it important enough. In Session C you will look at the other two personal faculties, willing and personal development.

2 Improving your thinking

Thinking is a skill, like any other, which can be learned and improved upon by practice and using the right tools.

2.1 Thinking at work

> 'Thinking is the most unhealthy thing in the world, and people die of it just as they die of any other disease. Fortunately thought is not catching.'
> Oscar Wilde.

In the past relatively few people were employed for their ability to think. Workers were called 'hands' as this was the only part of them seen as relevant to their work. Phrases such as 'you are not paid to think' can still be heard in some organizations, and terms such as 'intellectual', 'theoretical' or 'academic' are still often used as terms of abuse. But in most organizations this has changed or is changing. As organizations become flatter and responsibility is more devolved, for most supervisors, team leaders or first line managers making decisions and solving problems are central parts of their work. Decisions and problems demand thinking.

Session B

Activity 7

3 mins

Do you recognize that you have a 'thinking role' in your work? How comfortable are you with this role?

I understand and am comfortable with the role. However, 'quality thinking' requires 'quality' time which I don't always set aside.

Taking on responsibility for decisions and problems can be daunting for many people whose experience at school may have discouraged them from thinking of themselves as 'clever' or 'thinkers'. But nearly everybody has the 'mental equipment' to think clearly and deeply about their work, and anyone can improve their thinking with practice. The most important thing is to get rid of any beliefs such as 'I am not very bright'.

> **EXTENSIONS 1 AND 2**
> If you want to go further into these topics, look at *Lateral Thinking for Management* by Edward De Bono and *Use Your Head* by Tony Buzan.

There are of course techniques to help with problem solving and decision making and you will find some of these in the workbook in this series entitled *Solving Problems*. Here we have selected a few of the areas of thinking where many people find they can improve.

2.2 Observation and concentration

> 'I can never bring you to realize the importance of sleeves, the suggestiveness of thumb-nails, or the great issues that may hang from a boot-lace.'
> Sherlock Holmes (Sir Arthur Conan Doyle)

The basic building blocks of thinking are observation (do you really see what is about you?) and concentration (can you stay with one topic long enough to develop a train of thought?). A lot of the time we tend to drift through a situation looking, but without really seeing. A lot of the time we 'see' what we expect to see, without really checking that reality actually matches our expectations. This is especially likely if the situation is a highly familiar one: your normal place of work, the weekly team meeting, and so on. It is as if we are day-dreaming or half asleep: our bodies may be present but our minds are elsewhere.

In contrast, if we are observant we notice the small details that may be vital clues to some issue we should be attending to. Observation is 'looking with the brain in gear'. Observation does not take place in a vacuum, we do not simply 'observe'. Observation is guided by the questions we have; the more questions we have the better our observation.

Session B

Activity 8

5 mins

Look at one of your normal working situations through the eyes of somebody who is totally unfamiliar with this situation – a visitor to your organization perhaps. What might they see that you usually overlook (e.g. unwashed coffee cups, dried-out pot plants . . .)? What questions might they have about what they see (e.g. why is this place such a mess?)?

[handwritten response] My desk covered with unorganised papers, filing which means unfiled. E-mail box remaining uncleared. Am I really this disorganised? Are my priorities wrong? Aren't I making work for myself.

It is often difficult to concentrate at work because of the many interruptions. But even without these outer obstacles it can be hard to concentrate.

Activity 9

5 mins

Choose a moment at work or at home when you know you will not be interrupted for five minutes. Take a familiar object such as a pencil, spoon or paper clip. Try to stay fully concentrated on this object for five minutes. Consider what it is made from, where it was made, how it was made, who might have first invented it, and so on. At the end of five minutes award yourself a mark out of ten for how well you stayed concentrating on your object.

Even without anyone else interrupting you, you probably found that you consistently interrupted yourself, as your thoughts strayed from the object and unconnected ideas entered your mind. Both observation and concentration rely on 'mental muscles' that get flabby from underuse. But these muscles can be strengthened through exercise.

Session B

Activity 10

35 mins

Plant a crocus or daffodil bulb (or something similar) in a pot. When it sprouts, make a new sketch of it every day for a week. Spend only about five minutes making your sketch. Try to notice how your observation of the bulb changes over the week. Also notice if your powers of concentration change. At the end of the week, put your sketches side by side in time order and observe how the plant has developed day by day. (Optional extra: If you want to get the full benefit from this Activity, continue right through the growth, flowering and decay of the plant.)

2.3 Common biases in thinking

There are a number of common biases that you should look out for in the ways you use information in your thinking:

- Selective attention: as noted in the discussion of observation, people have a tendency to attend to information they expect or want. Less expected or desired information is often ignored.
- Order effects: people have a tendency to pay more attention to information they receive first or last. Information in the middle tends to get overlooked.
- Overconfidence in own experience: people tend to overvalue information based on their own experience, when a wider sample of experience would suggest something different. For example, a couple of bad experiences with a supplier might lead to the conclusion 'this is a poor supplier', when actually these were not typical and if all the evidence were considered the supplier might be judged a good one.
- Difficulty in changing one's mind: once people have formed a view they tend to hold onto it, even if later evidence suggests they should revise their opinion.
- Ease of availability: people tend to rely on information that is readily available, ignoring other potentially valuable sources which are more difficult to get at.
- Valuing according to source: people often assess the reliability of information according to who supplies it. This allows personal dislikes and prejudices to come into play.

Session B

Activity 11

15 mins

Think of a decision you have made at work which went wrong in some way, for example a purchasing or recruitment decision that you later regretted. Was this faulty decision due to any biases in your usage of information? Did you, for example:

- fail to use information that was available if you had looked?
- only use part of the information that you did have?
- wrongly assess information because of who gave it to you or because of your expectations or wishes?
- make your mind up too early?

You may find it useful to do this Activity with one or more of your colleagues as it is not always easy to look objectively at one's own decisions.

[handwritten response]

The best ways to avoid these biases are:

- to be aware of your own tendencies
- to check your thinking with someone else who is sufficiently knowledgeable and can be relied on not to be influenced by you. This person will almost certainly have their own biases, but hopefully their biases will be different from yours and may cancel them out.

2.4 Helicopter vision and ways of looking

An important capacity in thinking is what some people call 'helicopter vision'. This has been defined as 'The ability to rise above the particulars of a situation and perceive it in its relations to the overall environment'.[1] It could also be called, 'seeing the wood for the trees'. Connected with helicopter vision – and a way in which you can practise this kind of thinking – is more generally to practise looking at things and situation in different ways. Here are four ways that it can be useful to think about a situation, using a classroom as the example.

---

[1] Handy, C. *Understanding Organizations*. Penguin, 3rd Edition, 1985, page 95.

Session B

- Form – what it looks like. Here you are concerned with physical appearances. A classroom typically contains desks and chairs in lines for the children with a larger desk and blackboard for the teacher at the front. There may be a map of the world on the wall, paintings done by the children, and so on.

- State – what it is doing. A maths class may be in progress.

- Function – how it operates. The teacher writes on the blackboard (for example) and asks the children questions about what has been written. The children make notes in their exercise books.

- Purpose – why it exists. To educate children, to relieve parents of their child-minding responsibilities . . .

Looking at things in these different ways can help open up new possibilities in your thinking. The same physical object, machine, setting can be used to achieve different purposes. (The children's classroom can be used in the evening for the local band to practise . . .) The same purpose can be achieved in different physical ways (children could be educated by correspondence courses, via the Internet . . .)

Activity 12 (8 mins)

Think of an object, machine or situation at work. Describe it physically, the states it can be in, how it works, what its purpose is. What other uses could your example have? In what other ways could the purpose of your example be achieved?

A computer (PC) sitting on my desk & linked to a printer. Takes up space, can be a distraction. To help with communication, preparation of paperwork, filing etc. By using a keyboard (functions of some keys still a mystery).

2.5 Imagination and intuition

Thinking is of course about making logical use of the facts available to you about some existing situation, problem or issue. But thinking is also about how things could be, in other words, imagination. Imagination is often dismissed ('it's only your imagination'), but if you are going to go beyond what **is** to what **could be**, then you have to imagine. In the last Activity when you thought about novel uses for your example or other ways you could achieve the same purpose, you were using imagination.

Session B

> Einstein said that he began to get the ideas for his theory of relativity by imagining while on a tram journey what it would look like to travel on a beam of sunlight.

Successful use of your imagination requires you to free yourself from your past and current experiences and all your preconceptions. You also have to free yourself from the linear style of thinking (going logically from one step to the next) and be willing to make jumps that have no 'logical' justification. Edward De Bono calls this shifting from vertical to lateral thinking.

> **EXTENSION 2**
> A useful technique here is the 'mindmap' described by Tony Buzan in *Use Your Head*.

The normal medium of our thinking is language and words are very good for logical, vertical thinking. Thinking more visually (imagination implies using **images**) can help us break out of our normal patterns. Sketches, diagrams, doodles can all help in this process.

Activity 13

10 mins

Students of organizations have often thought about places of work as if they were machines, organisms, military units, computers, political systems and the like. Describe your place of work (or some aspect of it) by completing the following sentence in terms of **one** of the following: a machine; an animal; a plant; or some other image of your choosing (e.g. unexploded bomb, a theatrical performance, a busy station in the rush hour ...):

My place of work is like .. *a busy road junction with traffic coming from all directions and only brief lulls in between.*

What aspect of your place of work does your image emphasize (e.g. its lack of humanity, chaos, excitement ...)? Does your choice of image tell you anything about what you should do to improve your place of work (e.g. an 'unexploded bomb' may be defused, a 'machine' may need some human warmth ...)?

Illustrates to a certain extent the order out of chaos but equally the relentless pressure. It is only relieved by brief periods of calm before inevitable interruption starts "the traffic" once again.

Session B

Another kind of thinking which is often neglected in working life is intuition. John Adair describes intuition as follows:

Intuition is the power or faculty of immediately apprehending that something is the case. Apparently it is done without intervention of any reasoning process. There is no deductive or inductive step-by-step reasoning, no conscious analysis of the situation, no employment of imagination – just a quick and ready insight – 'I just know'.[2]

Often we are suspicious of our intuitions. Sometimes we ignore our intuition, and regret it later. Although it can appear that some people are more naturally intuitive than others, it may be that all people have the capacity, but 'intuitive' people are better at hearing what their intuition has to say and then trusting this intuition.

2.6 Feeding your thinking

> 'I consider that a man's brain originally is like a little empty attic, and you have to stock it with such furniture as you choose.' Sherlock Holmes (Sir Arthur Conan Doyle)

As well as practice, thinking needs 'feeding'. This means ensuring that your thinking receives a good diet of fresh experiences, ideas, facts, examples, and so on. If you limit your diet to the same old experiences and take in no new intellectual content, then your thinking will have little to work on. Your diet should not only include things directly relevant to your work, but also things that may seem to have only marginal connection to your working life. Many important breakthroughs have come about when somebody put together two or more ideas that might have been around for some time, but nobody had connected before.

Activity 14 (3 mins)

How do you currently feed your thinking? Is this a nourishing diet?

- Training and professional development
- Networking
- Links with others within management.

---

[2] Adair, J. *Effective Decision Making*. Pan, 1985, page 92.

Session B

There are many ways you can feed your thinking. Here are a few examples:

- Going to exhibitions, conferences, and the like
- Going on training courses
- Visiting other organizations engaged in similar or related work to your own
- Reading directly work-related newspapers, magazines, books and journals
- Reading a magazine which generally informs and challenges you (e.g. *New Scientist*, *The Economist*, *Time*)
- Talking with friends about their work
- Watching/listening/reading more informative programmes/articles on/in the television/radio/newspapers

3 Working with your feelings

While there are many books aimed at people at work on thinking and willing (usually described as 'motivation'), there are very few on feelings. Emotion often seems to be the great unacknowledged dimension of working life. Many managers pride themselves on their 'rationality' and 'objectivity'. Any admission that they actually have feelings would be interpreted as 'I am not always as rational or objective as I like to think I am.'

But of course everybody has feelings whether they admit it or not. The trouble is that feelings which are not openly expressed continue to work away under the surface where they cannot be dealt with.

3.1 The proper place of feelings at work

'Feelings at work' might seem an unikely idea in many work places but let us explore it further.

Activity 15 (3 mins)

What feelings do you most commonly experience at work? When do these feelings arise? Do you display these feelings?

- Apprehension in anticipation of challenges
- Pleasure in celebrating the success of others

Session B

Feelings, like thinking, help us orient ourselves in the world in which we live and work. Discovering that we like or dislike something, that it makes us happy or sad, angry, frustrated or afraid, is essential in knowing what we should approach or avoid or do something about. There are things which should make us angry; this may generate the energy needed to tackle something that should be tackled. There are things we should be afraid of, so that we steer clear of danger.

Trouble arises when feelings are either suppressed or are inappropriate to the situation. We often talk about feelings being 'bottled up'. These feelings build up and up, until some minor remark or incident triggers the release of all these feelings in a great explosion of emotion. The poor person who has unwittingly detonated this explosion finds themselves caught up in a great wave of anger or grief that seems out of all proportion to the 'cause'. Some people are so successful at suppressing their feelings that they never let them out at all. There is plenty of evidence that this can lead to physical illness.

Feelings can be inappropriate when we transfer feelings that belong to one place to another, or from an earlier time in our lives to a later one. A common experience is carrying feelings from home to work, or the other way round. This does not usually matter when the feelings are light (happiness, joy, and so on), but does when the feelings are dark or heavy (anger, depression, frustration, and so on).

Activity 16

5 mins

- 'When I first came into this company I had to deal a lot with the manager of another related project. I found myself dreading these meetings. I had huge feelings of inferiority and sometimes was almost lost for words. I just couldn't understand what was happening, because this manager actually treated me perfectly well. It was only after some time that I suddenly realized there was something about his looks and manner that reminded me of a headmaster at a school I was at when I was eleven or twelve, with whom I had had a lot of problems and who had given me a very hard time. Once I realized what was behind my discomfort with this project manager, I was able to manage my feelings much better. I could never completely dispel the feelings of unease, but I could at least stop them interfering excessively in our working relationship.' Brian, team leader in a software company.

Have you had similar experiences to Brian? Did you realize where your feelings originated? Could you keep these feelings from affecting your work?

[handwritten response]

Session B

3.2 Managing your feelings

People often say 'control your feelings' meaning 'suppress them, do not let your feelings show'. But controlling should mean using and expressing your feelings in ways that are constructive without letting them run away with you. This could be better described as 'managing your feelings'. Here are some guidelines on how you can manage your feelings:

- **Express your feelings in the moment.** Working life tends to be full of minor irritations and frustrations. If you express your irritation, frustration or anger in the moment it arises, then you can let it out in a controlled manner. If you let these feelings accumulate, then as discussed above, they may come out in an uncontrolled blow-up, perhaps at an inappropriate time. In many working situations, it may feel that to express your feelings is to take a risk. But in fact other people will usually sense what you are really feeling and in the long term they are more likely to respect your honesty in saying what you feel, rather than in attempting to keep up a mask.

- **Practise giving a 'feelings commentary'.** Studies have shown that a valuable technique used by skilled negotiators is the feelings commentary. This technique can be used in all kinds of situation and means telling the other person what you are feeling without acting out that feeling. For example, a negotiator may be angry at some tactic adopted by the other side. But to get angry may put a delicate negotiation at risk. So the skilled negotiator may say (calmly but forcefully), 'What you are doing is making me angry. If you carry on behaving like that, we cannot go on doing business together.'

- **Find a way to release feelings you cannot express at work.** There will inevitably be situations at work where it is just not possible to let your feelings out or even express them via a feelings commentary. Usually the most immediate need is to find a time and place where you can calm down on your own. Often it is a good idea to try to let out the energy built up through a strong emotion. Physically demanding sports can help here. Squash is a good example; the act of hitting something hard can be a wonderful release. A good form of 'first aid' is to scream and shout in the car (traffic and presence of other road users permitting). For many people some kind of artistic pursuit can also be a way they can express their feelings.

- **Feed your feeling life.** The feeling life needs 'feeding', just like the thinking life. Children have very rich feeling lives, but many people find as they grow up they lose touch with their feelings. They often live in very restricted 'emotional spaces'. They limit themselves to a handful of 'safe' feelings and exclude feelings which seem 'unpleasant' or 'dangerous'. The price paid for this is a loss of vast areas of human experience and a vague sensation of not being fully alive. Music, novels, films, painting, and so on can all be food for the feeling life. But it is important not to restrict yourself to a diet that reinforces the feelings you are comfortable with (e.g. books and films with happy endings), but to try to experience the full range of human feelings.

Session B

- **Take responsibility for your feeling life.** Many people do not like to be responsible for their own feelings. If something makes them sad or angry or upset, then they blame this feeling on somebody else. Similarly, they often look to somebody else to make them proud, happy or joyful. But nobody else can be responsible for our feelings, only ourselves. We have to take ownership of our own feelings, and say 'If I don't like the way I am feeling, only I can do something to change it.' In a curious way we have to learn to be objective about our own feelings, to ask ourselves 'What does this feeling tell me about my situation? What does it tell me about myself? What do I want to do about it?'

3.3 Looking at your values

Values are something about which you feel strongly and they affect all your actions and beliefs – at work as much as anywhere else.

Activity 17 (5 mins)

Look at the list below and tick the **five** items that are most important to you:

- Being wealthy
- Having a close family life
- Being respected by your colleagues
- Your company being successful
- Having exotic holidays
- Having a satisfying sex life
- Having a challenging job
- Having security
- Having time to pursue your leisure interests/hobbies
- Protecting the environment
- Having plenty of friends
- Your children being happy
- Your partner being happy
- Good relations with your team
- Good relations with your boss
- Freedom to make your own decisions
- .... (anything else you want to include)
- .... (anything else you want to include)
- .... (anything else you want to include)

Session B

The items in this list can all be considered as values. Values are closely connected with feelings, because we value what we feel to be good or important. Thinking of course can play a part in values, but fundamentally the choice whether you value your children's happiness more or less than having plenty of friends comes down to what you feel about each one. It may seem that this is a rather odd choice to have to make, but in practice we have to make choices like this all the time. We only have so much time, energy, money and other resources. Our values determine where we spend these resources. If we choose to spend our time with our children, we have less time to spend with our friends.

There is often a mismatch between what people say are their values and what their actions suggest their values deep down actually are. What they say can be called people's 'espoused values' and what they do their 'values-in-action'.

Activity 18

5 mins

- 'I always felt that I valued having a really stimulating job and used to tell all my friends how boring I found my present job. But when I was offered the job of managing the whole project, I realized that a stimulating job meant taking a lot of risks. The more I thought about it, I found that actually I valued the security of my current job much more than I was aware of. When pushed, I decided that security was more important to me than stimulation, and so I turned the job down.' Karen, first line manager in a pharmaceutical company.

Go back to the list in the last Activity and, using a different colour, tick the five values which you actually pursue most actively in terms of your time, energy, money, and so on. Are there any mismatches between your espoused values and your values-in-action? Were you aware of these mismatches? Do these arise from your free choice, or are they somehow imposed on you?

Mismatches arise from a combination of free choice and impositions which I'm aware of.

As you have seen, values provide a bridge between feelings and actions. In the next session, you will explore the motives underlying your actions more closely.

Session B

Self-assessment 2

10 mins

For questions 1 to 7 complete the sentences with a suitable word or words from the following list:

| FEELINGS | INTUITION | CONCENTRATION | VALUES |
| IMAGINATION | OBSERVATION | LATERAL | THINK |

1 Employees are no longer simply hands, nowadays everyone has to _think_.

2 The foundations of good thinking are _observation_ and _concentration_.

3 If you want to picture how things could be, you must use your _imagination_.

4 _Intuition_ is the faculty that gives us the answer, without having worked it out through logic and analysis.

5 Edward De Bono invented the term '_lateral_ thinking'.

6 People's _values / feelings_ are often overlooked or neglected at work.

7 The things in life that are important to us are our personal _values_.

8 Give three examples of common biases in thinking:
   selectivity
   availability
   confidence in experience

9 What are four ways of looking at a situation that are helpful in developing 'helicopter vision'?
   form
   function
   state
   reason/purpose

28

Session B

10 Which of the following are helpful in managing your feelings?

- Bottle up your emotions
- Express your feelings in the moment
- Never admit to being angry or sad
- Practise giving a feelings commentary
- Shout at anybody who gets in your way
- Drink a lot of alcohol
- Find a way to release feelings that you cannot express at work
- Blame others for how you are feeling
- Feed your feeling life
- Take responsibility for your feeling life

Answers to these questions can be found on pages 60–1.

4 Summary

- In most organizations today everybody must be willing to think about their work.

- Observation implies really seeing – looking and thinking.

- Concentration means staying consistently with a line of thinking.

- Observation and concentration can be improved with practice.

- People are vulnerable to a range of biases in their thinking. These can be minimized by self-awareness and checking one's thinking processes.

- Helicopter vision and practising thinking about things from different perspectives can improve the quality of thinking.

- Imagination and intuition are both valuable ways of going beyond the limitations of logical, analytic thinking.

- Thinking needs to be 'fed'.

- Feelings are a legitimate part of working life when expressed appropriately.

- Feelings need to be managed.

- Values are concerned with what we feel to be good or bad, important or unimportant.

Session C Personal drive and personal development

1 Introduction

In the last session you looked at your thinking and your management of your emotions. But while clear or creative thinking and proper management of your feelings are necessary for effectiveness, they are not by themselves sufficient. Being effective is ultimately about achieving things, and this requires you to be able to motivate yourself, to drive yourself into action. So in this session you look at how you can increase your personal drive.

Improving your self-management in the areas of thinking, emotions and personal drive is about more than the simple acquisition of new skills or techniques. Improvement at these deeper levels of self-management requires changes in the kind of person you are, what is often called personal development. The second part of this session explores what is meant by personal development, describes how learning and change are the core skills in development, and introduces ways in which you can make personal development activities central to your life.

2 Harnessing your personal drive

As you have seen, being effective depends on having the right knowledge and skills for the task in hand and organizing yourself to apply them, through, for example, sound time management. These are all topics covered elsewhere in the Super Series 3 workbooks. But effectiveness depends not only on knowing how to achieve a task, it also depends on your **wanting** to achieve this task. However much you know and however skilful you are, this counts for little if you do not want to make something happen.

2.1 What motivates you?

This concerns your personal drive. Personal drive is a mixture of how much you want to do something (what was referred to earlier as your will) and how much energy you have to put into the task. Concepts closely related to personal drive are willpower or self-motivation. You will look at personal energy shortly, but first we look at the question of what you want.

Session C

Activity 19

10 mins

- 'A couple of years back the cricket club I belong to decided to build a new pavilion. We were still using the old Home Guard shed from the Second World War and this was now too small and falling down. It was a lot of work. I took on the fund raising and organized raffles, jumble sales and all sorts of events. To save money we agreed to knock down the old pavilion and lay the foundations for the new one ourselves, so the builder simply had to erect the new building. This was also a lot of work, and meant we all had to give up a number of weekends. But everybody joined in and nobody complained. What I found funny when I thought about it was that I actually worked far harder for this new pavilion than I ever work in my job – and far from getting paid for it, it was actually costing me money!' Mike, supervisor in a telecommunications company.

Think of two or three examples from your life – at work or outside work – where you have really put a lot of effort into achieving something. What made you want to do these things so much? Do you have similar levels of commitment to your present work?

[handwritten response:]
- positive outcomes · rewards (personal/emotional)
- feel good · recognition of job well done
- lack of direction in present circumstances pending reshaping of service

Much thinking in business is about how to motivate people through the promise of what could be called 'external rewards': pay rises, promotion, trips to 'sales conferences' in exotic locations, and so on. But in doing the last Activity you may well have found that when you are deeply committed to doing something it is often because you see it as being worthwhile. Something is worthwhile for you if it is consistent with your 'inner values' that you explored in Session B. Work which is consistent with your values is likely to feel meaningful; work which is not consistent will probably feel meaningless.

This is not to say that things like money are not important at work, of course they are. But in the long run external rewards are unlikely to keep you effective if your work seems meaningless or conflicts with your values. An important consequence is that the more you work out of your inner values rather than in pursuit of external rewards, the more you have a sense of being master of your own destiny and not simply responding to forces outside of you. You will be proactive – taking initiative and responsibility – rather than reactive – letting events drive you.

Session C

2.2 Working with the tension between current reality and the ideal

If you look at people who have really made significant contributions to human life, whether in business, politics, science, art, or any other sphere of activity, you usually find that they were motivated by more than material success. They typically perceived a gap between some aspect of how things are and how they would like them to be. They had a strong experience of the tension between current reality and the ideal. 'Ideal' here does not mean something wonderful but probably unobtainable, but rather something which is derived from ideas about how things could be better. Once again, your definition of 'better' will depend on your personal values.

For example, Henry Ford saw that ordinary people could not afford to own a car. But he had ideas about how to develop a system of mass production that would make cars affordable for the many rather than the few. He was motivated not solely by the wish to make money, but also by the belief that widespread car ownership was a desirable aim. His aim was ideal but also highly practical.

Activity 20 — 10 mins

Using the following table note down **three** examples of areas to do with your work where you can see improvements could be made. For each example describe briefly how things are (current reality) and how you think things could/should be (ideal). Examples might be customer needs which are not being met, wasteful work practices, poor interpersonal relationships, or any other area you like. In thinking about how things should be, consider how your ideal expresses your personal values. Ask yourself if you would be willing to:

- expend effort and maybe other resources to bring your ideal about;
- accept risks that might be involved (e.g. loss of goodwill from colleagues, disapproval from senior management . . .).

Example	Current reality	Your ideal
1. Consultation approach to clients	Apprehension about not giving client what they want	Welcoming consultation as a positive contribution to service delivery
2. Budget Management	Working with old budget centres	Better grouping of items to budget for
3.		

33

Session C

Note that although the focus here is on your personal drive, the last Activity also engaged your thinking (can you perceive and think about current reality clearly? can you imagine how things could be?) and your emotions (how do you feel about current reality and your ideal?).

2.3 Circles of concern and circles of influence

> **EXTENSION 3**
> An essential read if you are serious about becoming more effective is *The Seven Habits of Highly Effective People* by Stephen Covey.

Personal drive is about taking action where you see action is necessary or desirable. But you may see many such areas. In choosing where to focus, Stephen Covey makes a useful distinction between 'circles of concern' and 'circles of influence'. These are shown in the figure below.

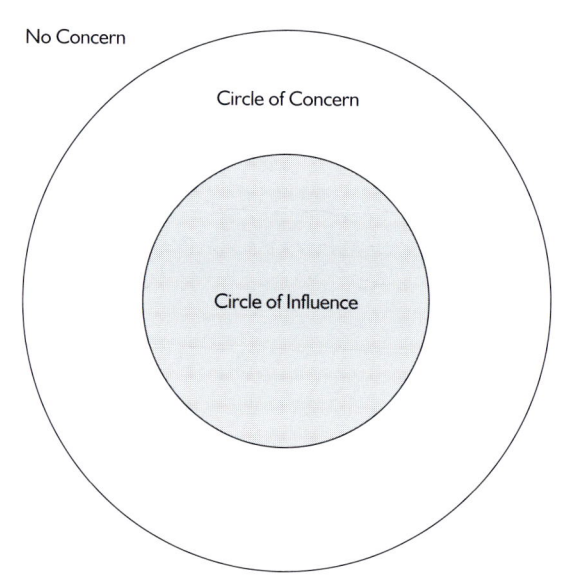

No Concern

Circle of Concern

Circle of Influence

Circles of Concern and and Influence (from Stephen R. Covey, *The Seven Habits of Highly Effective People*)

Outside of both circles are issues which are of no concern or interest to you. Within the outer circle are issues which are of concern to you, they are issues you would like to do something about. Issues which are within the inner circle are both of concern to you and under your influence, at least to some extent. If you are being effective you are directing your personal drive towards those issues that are within your Circle of Influence. If you are spending a lot of time and energy on issues that are within your Circle of Concern but not within your Circle of Influence, then you are probably being ineffective.

Session C

Activity 21

3 mins

Look again at the three examples you chose in the last Activity. Does each one lie in your Circle of Influence? Or only in your Circle of Concern?

All fall in both

2.4 Acting ethically

If effectiveness is about getting the right things done in a business sense, ethics is about doing the right thing in a moral sense. Ethical questions may come up in connection with the end result of your work; is the product or service a 'good' one? Goodness of course tends to be in the eye of the beholder. Some people find certain activities intrinsically not right; for example, the manufacture of weapons, the distribution of pornography, the building of nuclear power stations, or the export of live animals. Others find these perfectly acceptable. There may also be ethical questions arising from **how** the work is done. For example, many people would see ethical issues in work that involves environmental pollution, risks to health and safety, deception, cruelty to animals, discrimination, and so forth.

Some ethical boundaries are laid down by law, by industry regulations, or by professional codes of conduct. But there are many products, services and practices which may not violate any laws, regulations or codes of conduct, but which nonetheless raise ethical issues. In dealing with these moral 'grey areas', you have to rely on your own personal principles and values. The clearer you can be about what you believe to be important, the easier (or better said, the less difficult) it is for you to take your own position on tricky ethical issues. Clarity about your principles and values makes it easier to resist pressure which may be placed on you to act in ways you consider to be unethical.

Session C

Activity 22

Portfolio of evidence C1.1

20 mins

This Activity may provide the basis of appropriate evidence for your S/NVQ portfolio. It will also help you to develop an ethical perspective to your work.

Use the table below to review the ethical issues you face in your work.

List below **three** ethical issues to do with your work. These may be issues to do with your product or service, or to do with way the work is carried out	For each issue note down any laws, regulations or codes of conduct which define what is permitted or acceptable	For each issue note down **your** personal values which are involved (e.g. the well-being of children is paramount; the environment must be protected; all dealings with clients must be based on honesty . . .)
Issue 1: *Client confidentiality.*		
Issue 2:		
Issue 3:		

Answer the following questions about **one** of the issues you have listed above which is especially difficult for you:

- Does this issue arise because of a conflict between your personal values and the values of your organization?
- What do you see as the implications for the people affected by this issue? (E.g. customers get a bad deal, staff have to behave dishonestly, the environment is damaged . . .)
- Do you actively confront this issue? If so, how?
- Are you put under pressure to behave non-ethically?
- Are there sources of support you could turn to to help you resist these pressures?
- What could you do to contribute to creating a more ethical culture in your organization?

Session C

2.5 Releasing energy

We said earlier that personal drive depends on knowing what you want and having the energy to do it. If you know what you want and want it strongly enough, then usually this has the effect of releasing the energy you need, possibly energy you were not even aware you had. But sometimes the energy does not seem to be there. An effect of prolonged stress, for example, is that your energy reserves slowly but surely get used up. You can find more about stress and energy depletion, and what to do about it, in *Managing Tough Times* in this series.

Another problem directly connected with the theme of this workbook is that often our thinking, feeling and willing are not all pulling in the same direction. Our thoughts may tell us to do one thing about a situation, our feelings tell us to do something different, and we may want to do neither. In such moments we are divided within ourselves, and our different kinds of energy work against, rather than with each other. Psychologists call such states being 'incongruent'. On the other hand, when our thoughts, feelings and actions are all consistent with each other, then this is being 'congruent'.

Activity 23 (5 mins)

'I once had to consider dismissing one of my team. I could see that the logic of the situation at work demanded this. She could not do the job and all my efforts to get her to improve had failed. But I felt deeply uncomfortable with the thought of her being sacked. I knew she was a single parent and depended very much on this job to support her family. I did not want her to worry and so I did not tell her of my doubts about her future in this job, although I felt this was wrong too. Part of me did not want her to stay as she was reducing the overall team performance, but another part of me could not bring myself to sack her. I tried to get my boss to make the decision, but she kept passing it back to me, saying it was my responsibility.' Mohinder, first line manager in a plastics company.

Do you think Mohinder was being congruent or incongruent? Was he being effective? What could he do to change the situation?

Incongruent and thus ineffective. Talk to boss about possible change of job ie to another. Talk with team member and share anxieties and look at any other options.

37

Session C

In this example we see the opposite of strong personal drive: paralysis. Mohinder can only get out of his impasse by working to become clear about his thinking, feeling, values and desires. Can he really see the situation clearly? What are the consequences for customers, the team, for the company and for himself of keeping a person who cannot contribute to the work? Could he be putting the jobs of others at risk through compromising the effectiveness of the team? What does it mean for the person herself to stay in a job for which she is so unsuited? Are there other options he has not thought about? What are his values in relation to the problem person, the rest of the team, customers, the company? What does he want: a quiet life? an effective team? to escape his responsibilities? Only by working through these questions and others like them, can Mohinder expect to achieve congruence, and thereby find the energy to take constructive action.

3 Changing yourself

The theme of this workbook has been that effective management of other people, resources, money, information and so on depends on effective management of yourself.

3.1 Making yourself the focus of action

> Personality is less a finished product than a transitive process. While it has some stable features, it is at the same time continually undergoing change. Gordon W. Allport, *'Becoming'*.

To become effective and to stay effective usually means changing yourself. This is not simply change but development. Mike Pedler and Tom Boydell describe what this means.

[Development] might be a new skill; a new way of seeing things; a new attitude; or a new set of feelings; a new level of consciousness or mode of managing. The important word in all of these is *new*. Development is not just more of something that you have already; it is not just an increase in knowledge, or a higher degree of an existing skill. Development is a *different* state of being or functioning, rather than a mere topping up of something that you already have.

EXTENSION 4
Managing Yourself by Mike Pedler and Tom Boydell is a comprehensive book covering most areas of effectiveness.

One way you can think of personal development is in terms of the Circles of Concern and Influence you looked at earlier. You can think of personal development as increasing the size of your Circle of Influence so that it covers more of your Circle of Concern. In this final part of the workbook you can explore how you can make personal development a central part of your working life (and beyond).

Session C

3.2 Your personal vision

> 'Life is what happens when you have planned something else.' Anon, quoted by Scott Peck in *The Different Drum*.

Earlier in this session, you saw that personal drive can come from an awareness of the gap between some state of current reality and some future state that you consider desirable. This same idea can apply to yourself as well as to states of affairs in your work. An awareness of how you actually are compared with how you would like to be, can provide the motive force for self-development.

Activity 24 (15 mins)

You may sometimes have thought about future goals in terms of career planning: where you would like to be in two, five or ten years' time, say. But in this Activity you can go deeper than just thinking about the kind of job you want to do; you can think about the kind of person you want to be. Imagine you have now reached retirement age. Write a brief description of how you would like to be remembered by your former colleagues at work. What achievements would you like to be remembered for? What contributions would you like to have made? How do you want others to think of you as a person?

[Handwritten response: Being effective but fair, never asking people to do things I wouldn't do. Being supportive with a touch of coercion. Building up a strong team and valuing their work. Someone who listens, doesn't ignore opinions but equally is prepared to make decisions and stick with them unless reasoned argument suggests otherwise.]

By comparing the ideal picture of yourself you can begin to identify those areas which you want to be the points of focus of your personal development activities.

3.3 Moving towards your vision

> **EXTENSION 5**
> *The Fifth Discipline* by Peter Senge. Chapter 9, 'Personal Mastery' is especially relevant.

You may well experience an overwhelming sense that the gap between what you would like to be and how you are is too wide to ever be bridged. Peter Senge in *The Fifth Discipline* (Extension 5) remarks that two common feelings when confronting one's personal vision are powerlessness ('I cannot change') and unworthiness ('I do not deserve to change'). These feelings usually have their roots in early childhood and are notoriously difficult to overcome. But the beginning of development lies in accepting the challenge

Session C

of personal growth. Out of the experience that one can change comes the discovery that one is not powerless. There is often a liberating feeling that one can take charge of one's own destiny. This in turn can lead to more and more positive experience of one's self that slowly builds one's self-esteem.

There are some general principles that should be followed on the path of self-development. The ones given below are based on suggestions from Scott Peck.[3]

Accept responsibility. If you do not take responsibility for your own development, you can be pretty sure that nobody else will.

> 'Know thyself.'
> Inscription on the Oracle of Apollo at Delphi, Greece (sixth century BC)

Accept development takes time. It takes time in two senses. You must set time aside for your development. Without investment you will not see any return. But development also takes time in the sense of being a long, slow process. For long periods you may not notice any changes, no matter how much time and effort you put in. But eventually, when you look back over a stretch of time, you suddenly become aware that you are not the person you were, you have grown. Connected with this principle is the idea that you do not try to change everything about yourself at once. Start with small changes where the chances of success are good. Early success leads to a willingness to go on to bigger, more profound changes.

Be dedicated to reality. Senge describes this as 'commitment to the truth'. This requires an unflinching willingness to see yourself as you really are and the world as it really is. We all carry about 'mental maps'. These contain beliefs, assumptions, theories, opinions that help us find our way around the world (e.g. 'People are generally motivated by money'; 'Senior management is out of touch . . .'). They also contain all our beliefs about ourselves (e.g. 'I know everything about this business', 'I always try to be sympathetic', 'I am patient . . . likeable' . . .). The trouble is that the maps may get out of date. They may also have contained errors from the outset. We normally mistake our mental maps for reality and in fact we only become aware of our mental maps when we or the world no longer behaves in the way our map leads us to expect. A crisis usually has this effect. Recognizing that our map may be wrong in some respects can be profoundly disturbing; we literally lose our orientation. We can either pretend that it is our map that is correct (and the world that is wrong!) or we can take on the effort and pain of redrawing our maps of the world and especially ourselves.

Keep a sense of balance. This principle is necessary to counteract any negative side-effects of following the other principles. Balance means not taking responsibility for everything, but only for those things for which you are genuinely responsible. Balance means not becoming obsessed with personal development to the expense of all other areas of your work and life. Balance means knowing when you must accept for the moment your picture of reality to get things done. Balance means not changing your mental maps without question when someone challenges your beliefs and assumptions, but weighing up what they say for its truth.

---

[3] Peck, M.S. *The Road Less Travelled.* Simon & Schuster, 1978.

Session C

Activity 25

10 mins

> 'For several years I had been coasting along in my job. I felt I was good at my work, and could do most of it with one hand tied behind my back. When we found out the area manager's job was falling vacant, I was confident that I would be asked to take it on. It came as a real shock when one of the other FLMs – who I had always thought a bit of an idiot – was given the job. At first I was bitter and resentful and thought the senior managers were also stupid. But finally I plucked up the courage to talk to my manager about why I'd not got the job. He said that, although they knew how competent I was, they thought I had got complacent and did not show enough initiative for the area manager's post. I was livid and tried to argue why they were wrong. But later when I thought about it, I could see they did have a point. I am now trying to find ways to pick my performance up again, so that I can get back in the running for promotion.'
> Julie, FLM in a television rental company.

Think of an experience you have had like Julie not getting promoted. How did you react? Did you tend to blame others? With hindsight, do you think it would have been more productive to re-evaluate yourself?

Disappointment. Did blame anyone else but myself which led to a evaluation of where I was & what I would need to do to get where I wanted to be.

3.4 Learning processes in personal development

> 'We learn what is significantly new only through adventures. However, going into the unknown is invariably frightening.'
> M. Scott Peck, *The Different Drum.*

Personal development is essentially a special kind of learning process: learning about yourself. You will find in the Super Series 3 User Guide some practical advice on how to learn. But personal development is a particularly difficult kind of learning and it is worthwhile to look a bit more deeply at how you can support your personal development with different kinds of learning.

The first kind of learning is imitation, copying what somebody else does. This is how small children learn and it is highly effective. Even as adults we can imitate, although for adults it is usually a more conscious process. One study of successful managers in the US found that the only thing they had in common was they had all worked for a highly effective boss in their first job. In personal development you can find a person who has a skill you want to develop or who exemplifies a personal attribute you would like to have. By careful observation of this person you can gain clues as to how you can develop this skill or attribute. Reading biographies or autobiographies of people you admire can also be a source of ideas and inspiration for your own development.

41

Session C

The second kind of learning is instruction, the type of traditional learning where somebody deliberately tries to teach you knowledge or a skill. This tends not to work well with adult personal development. Personal development has to come from the inside to the outside, it cannot be passed from the outside to the inside. But what can work is some form of mentoring. Here you find a person who is willing to talk with you about your personal development. A good mentor will not try to 'teach' you, but will help you become clear about what the real issues are and encourage you to find your own way forward.

The third kind of learning is experiential. This is probably the most effective for personal development. But experience on its own does not automatically lead to learning. Learning only occurs when you actively engage your thinking, feeling and willing to 'harvest' the personal lessons from your experience. A good way of thinking about this is given by the experiential learning cycle in the figure below.

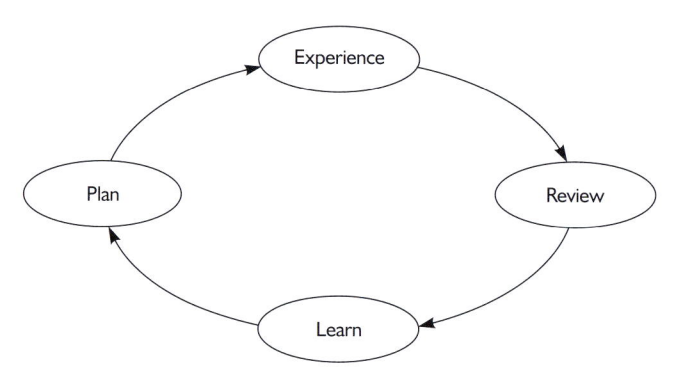

The experiential learning cycle.

As the name suggests, in the first phase of the cycle you start with an experience of some kind in the workplace. This is often a negative experience but can be positive. You try to observe this experience as actively as you can, 'with your brain in gear', as we said in Session B. In the second phase you review the experience. This means you try to 'stand outside' the experience, to look at it as an impartial observer might. You try to see what happened and why. You look for the consequences. In this phase you need to be dedicated to reality and especially to be totally honest about your own role in what happened.

In the third phase, you try to see what you can learn from your review:

'I should not have done that . . .'
'I misunderstood how that would work . . .'
'Perhaps if I had . . .'
'I need to learn more about . . .'

In the fourth and final phase, you plan how you are going to act in the future on the basis of what you have learned. The next time you find yourself in an appropriate situation, you put your plan into operation, observe the experience and start on another round of the cycle.

Session C

Remember that personal development is rarely about acquiring simple techniques. It is about changing deep-seated habits and attributes. This takes time and this means that you may have to go through the experiential learning cycle many times before you develop and master this new part of yourself.

Portfolio of evidence C1.1, C1.2

Activity 26

15 mins

This Activity may provide the basis of appropriate evidence for your S/NVQ portfolio. You will find a more detailed version of this Activity in the Work-based assignment later in the workbook.

Choose a recent experience at work from which you think you can learn something. Work through the four phases of the learning cycle and note down below what you have learned and what you would do differently next time such a situation arises.

Consultation with senior colleagues to maintain open communication even if and when there is likely to be disagreement – 'communicate, communicate, communicate!'

3.5 Finding support

As we have indicated, becoming more effective through working on yourself is difficult. It is especially difficult to do it on your own – the support of others can help you keep going when the effort seems too great and provide you with examples of things to do or try. An important feature of all these kinds of support is that you aim to give as well as receive support. The process of giving support can itself be highly developmental. We have already mentioned mentors, and here are some other ways you can get support:

Speaking partner. A mentor is usually someone older and more experienced than you. A speaking partner is more of an equal, somebody – a colleague or friend from outside work – with whom you have an agreement to discuss openly what you are trying to do, difficulties you are having and so on. Ideally the relationship is mutual, so that you help them as much as they help you.

Networking. This means building up a network of contacts (at work and beyond) of people who you have found have similar interests and aims to yourself. They are people you can talk to (as speaking partners) and can call on for help as you need. Of course they can also call on you.

Session C

Support group. Many people in recent years have found it helpful to belong to a support group of some kind. Support groups usually consist of six to twelve people who come together for two or three hours once a week or fortnight to share and discuss issues that they are facing in their lives. Some support groups focus on particular themes. For example, there are many 'women's groups', and more recently 'men's groups'. Other groups are organized around some common issue or interest.

3.6 Taking others into account

As you work to develop yourself, even if the changes are 'for the better', the people close to you (colleagues, partners, children, friends) may find what is happening to you disturbing. They may be confused or even threatened. Of course you are part of colleagues', family's and friends' own mental maps. They think they know you and can predict you (even your 'difficult' sides). You changing undermines their mental maps, and they are likely to need time to redraw the bit of their map which contains you. The key here is good communications, keeping the people who are important to you as informed as you can about what you are doing and why. This does not mean sharing everything, but it does mean letting them know about the process you are in.

4 Where do you go from here?

You are now approaching the end of this workbook. Through your work so far you should now be clearer about what you need to do to become more effective in your job. This workbook should have helped you make a start. But, as we have emphasized before, the kinds of deep changes that we have looked at here take time to bring about. You may have identified many areas in which you would like to change yourself. You may well feel daunted by the size of the task or be unsure where to begin. The important thing is that you do begin. You will find that in personal development everything is connected to everything else. As you work on one aspect of yourself, you will find that you naturally begin working on all the other aspects as well. In choosing where to begin, it is advisable to start on those areas where you think you will rapidly see benefits in your performance at work. Achieving visible results is the best way to ensure you keep on taking the time and trouble that personal development inevitably entails. The last Activity will help you decide where to begin.

Session C

Portfolio of evidence C1.1

Activity 27

45 mins

This Activity may provide the basis of appropriate evidence for your S/NVQ portfolio. It will also help you complete your Action plan later in the workbook.

Go back to Session A and look again at your results from the self-assessment questionnaires. Also look again at the figure on page 9 which summarizes the whole area covered by this workbook. Now, in the light of all your work on this workbook, complete the following:

1 The **three** things I most need to change about myself to increase my effectiveness at work are:

 1. *Develop technique to counter the longer/wider view*
 2. *Tighten up on monitoring effectiveness*
 3. *Develop skill in knowing when to delegate appropriately*

2 To bring these changes about the **three** things I most need to do are:

 1. *To allow myself some 'quality' thinking time.*
 2. *To build in time to focus on monitoring progress.*
 3. *Think carefully about what needs to be delegated and build in mechanisms to monitor job be done + how.*

3 When I have made these changes to myself, the **three** most obvious improvements in my work will be:

 A better overview of developments and my explanation / justification for them
 A more 'hands on' approach with colleagues + being there.
 A freeing up of some time because others are carrying out tasks I've done in the past.

Discuss your ideas listed above with your manager, possibly as part of your next performance appraisal. (If you have a mentor or speaking partner you could discuss your ideas with them as well as or possibly instead of your manager.) Note down below the main points that come out of these discussions.

 - performance management targets reflect a more hands on approach to monitoring. Used my pragmatic 'time management' to allow effective monitoring to take place.

As an optional, additional way of gathering evidence for your portfolio you might like to consider keeping a 'self development diary' for a period of time, say, two to three months. In this you could record all the events and experiences which give you opportunities for self-development, how you review these, the ideas for personal action you have arising from these events and experiences, what steps you actually take and what the consequences of these actions are.

Session C

Self-assessment 3

10 mins

For questions 1 to 6 complete the sentences with a suitable word or words from the following list:

INFLUENCE   CURRENT REALITY   VISION   ENERGY
EXTERNAL REWARD   IDEAL   CONCERN   WANT
CONGRUENT   INNER VALUES

1 Personal drive depends on how much you _want_ something and how much _energy_ you have.

2 Motivation can arise from _external reward_ but is better based on _inner values_.

3 Motivation to change something can arise from awareness of the gap between _current reality_ and a potential _ideal_ state of affairs.

4 Things we would like to do something about lie within our Circle of _Concern_, but things we can actually affect lie within our Circle of _Influence_.

5 When what we think, feel and want are consistent with each other, then we can be described as _congruent_.

6 Our picture of how we would like to be is our personal _vision_.

7 Which of the following are good principles for self-development:

- Expect others to do all the work for you
- ✓ Accept responsibility
- Expect instant results
- ✓ Accept development takes time
- Do not think about yourself; it is a self-indulgent waste of time
- ✓ Be dedicated to reality
- Reject everything others say about you as ill-informed or biased
- Concentrate of self-development to the exclusion of all else
- ✓ Keep a sense of balance

8 What are the four phases of the experiential learning cycle?

1 _experience_
2 _review/evaluation_
3 _lessons learnt_
4 _planning_

Answers to these questions can be found on pages 61–2.

Session C

5 Summary

- Putting knowledge and skills to good use requires personal drive.

- Personal drive needs you to want something and to have the energy to do what is necessary.

- Motivation based on inner values is usually stronger than that based on external rewards.

- Motivation for action can arise from awareness of a gap between current reality and how things could ideally be.

- Effective action needs us to distinguish between what is within our Circle of Influence and not merely within our Circle of Concern.

- Ethical issues may be defined by law, regulations or codes of conduct, but may also depend on personal values.

- We are at our most effective when our thinking, feeling and willing all work in harmony with each other.

- The drive for self-development can come from a well-developed personal vision of how we would like to be.

- There are reliable principles to follow in personal development.

- Personal development involves a special kind of learning. It may involve imitation, instruction or experiential learning.

- Experiential learning involves a four phase cycle: experience, review, learn and plan.

Performance checks

1 Quick quiz

Jot down the answers to the following questions on *Becoming More Effective*.

Question 1   What are the four main areas where a manager must be effective?
People
Resources
Information
Activities

Question 2   List three common 'outer obstacles' to effectiveness.
Time
Information
Skills

Question 3   Where do 'inner obstacles' to effectiveness originate?
Within the individual.

Question 4   What is meant by 'self-management'?
Use of personal resources to do job.

Question 5   What are the four main areas to be managed in self-management?
Feeling
Personal development
Thinking
Willing

Question 6   Give definitions of 'observation' and 'concentration' as used in this workbook.
Seeing what is around the manager
Thinking about a topic long enough to reach some conclusions.

49

Performance checks

Question 7 — List three common biases in thinking.
Common influence
Reluctance to change mind
Availability

Question 8 — What do you need to do to use imagination successfully?
Being creative by thinking beyond influences of past experience + preconceptions.

Question 9 — Identify three ways you can help manage your feelings.
Express them
Find other places when not possible @ work.
Feed your feelings.

Question 10 — Give an example of how values work in everyday life.
Offer direction to time and energy.

Question 11 — What do you need for strong personal drive?
Clarity about the direction you're taking and energy to get you there.

Question 12 — To be effective should you attend more to things in your Circle of Concern or your Circle of Influence?
Circle of Influence.

Question 13 — Are ethical issues solely a matter of law, regulations and codes of conduct?
No — may be also influenced by personal values beyond laws etc.

Question 14 — What are the four principles of personal development?
Taking responsibility
Realising things take time
Having a balanced view
Be realistic.

Question 15 — Which form of learning is usually most suited to personal development?
Learning from experience.

Answers to these questions can be found on pages 62–3.

Performance checks

2 Workbook assessment

Read this example of someone becoming aware of their need to become more effective and then answer the questions.

- Christine is in charge of the invoicing department of a medium-sized engineering company. She has been doing this job for three years. For the first two years everything went fine. But over the past year, Christine has noticed she is not on top of the job in the same way as she was earlier. She believes her manager suspects all is not well, although he has not said anything openly yet.

  Christine has found herself making silly mistakes, letting invoices with errors slip past her checks. Quite a few times one of her team has said something to her which needed her to take action, and she completely forgot about it. Christine has also been more irritable with her staff. More than once she has blamed one of the invoice clerks for her own mistakes. In the past she had good relations with all her team, but now they tend to avoid her as much as possible. Several times, when they should have brought problems to her, they did not, causing further problems.

  Although she still likes her job, Christine has found herself browsing through the newspapers looking at job advertisements. She half wonders if it is not time she made a change. When she left school she had wanted to be a nurse, but this was not possible at that time. She still has a vague yearning to work in one of the 'caring professions'.

  Christine feels that something has to happen but is not sure what to do.

Write down your answers to the following:

- Is Christine being effective?
- What do you think is the root cause of the problem?
- What strikes you about Christine's self-management?
- How do you think she should set about sorting out her situation?

Give the reasons behind your thinking. You can make any assumptions about Christine, her colleagues and her work that seem reasonable.

51

Performance checks

Portfolio of evidence C1.1
3 Work-based assignment

⏱ 60 mins

The time guide for this assignment gives you an approximate idea of how long it is likely to take you to write up your findings. You will find you need to spend some additional time gathering information, perhaps talking to colleagues and thinking about the assignment.

Your written response to this assignment may form the basis of useful evidence for your S/NVQ portfolio. It will also help you to develop your ability to manage personal learning and development.

The assignment is designed to help you demonstrate:

- your ability to take responsibility for meeting your own learning and development needs;
- your ability to seek feedback on performance to identify strengths and weaknesses;
- your ability to learn from your own mistakes and those of others;
- your ability to change your behaviour where needed as a result of feedback;
- your ability to reflect systematically on your own performance and modify your behaviour accordingly;
- your ability to develop yourself to meet the competence demand of changing situations;
- your ability to transfer learning from one situation to another.

What you have to do

In this assignment you use the experiential learning cycle you looked at in Session C. For this assignment think of some recent experience you have had of a situation you were closely involved with and in which something went wrong. The important thing is that it is a situation from which you think you can learn something. You are asked to analyse this situation and see what you can learn from the experience in the light of what you have read in this workbook.

The first step is to write two descriptions of the experience. First, describe what happened from the point of view of an outside observer. Second, describe what you were thinking, feeling and wanting as the situation developed:

- Were you thinking how the situation had developed, what the problem was, what courses of action were open to you?
- Was your thinking clear or confused?
- Were you feeling calm, excited, anxious, flustered, angry, irritated . . .?
- Did you want to take control, run away, sort the problem out, restore peace, hit somebody, blame somebody . . .?

52

Performance checks

The second step is to analyse why the situation arose and why it developed as it did. You may find it helpful to talk to any others who were involved in the situation. Ask them about their thoughts, feelings and actions. Also ask them about what they thought of your role in the situation. Use the following questions to guide you:

- Why did others do what they did?
- Why did you do what you did?
- Did you misread the situation?
- Should you have expressed your feelings or, conversely, restrained your feelings?
- Did you react inappropriately?
- Did you have the knowledge and skills demanded by the situation?
- Were you clear about what was important for you in the situation?
- Did you know what you wanted to do?
- Was what you wanted to do different from what you felt you should do?
- What were the consequences of what you did?

The third step is to note down what you could learn from the experience:

- How could you have better managed your thoughts, feelings and behaviour?
- What could you have done differently?

The fourth and final step is to note down what you will do as a result of what you have learned and what you will try to do differently next time such a situation arises. Note down any measures you need to take that would help you prepare for a similar situation, for example:

- Talking through with your mentor how to deal with ethical dilemmas.
- Practice in giving a feelings commentary rather than showing excessive anger.
- Exploring ways to be more creative in your thinking.
- Discussing with a speaking partner any problems in expressing or restraining your feelings.
- Discovering how members of your support group would deal with such a situation.

Your whole assignment report does not need to be more than two to four pages long.

Reflect and review

1 Reflect and review

Now that you have completed your work on *Becoming More Effective*, let us review our workbook objectives.

- You should be better able to understand what self-management is all about

Self-management is about using your personal qualities effectively in pursuit of work-related goals. We suggested that there is an 'outer layer' of knowledge and skills relating directly to the work you do. There is also an inner, self-management layer, which involves what we called core personal skills. These are thinking, feeling, willing and personal development. You may want to ask yourself:

- Do I understand fully the difference between thinking, feeling and willing?
- Do I know what is meant by personal development?

- You should be better able to assess how well you manage yourself

You assessed yourself at two levels. The first concerned the outer-directed knowledge and skills you need to manage activities, resources, people and information. Improving yourself here can be achieved via the other workbooks in this series. The second level of assessment involved looking at your self-management in terms of thinking, feeling and willing. The questions here are:

- Am I clear where I need to concentrate my efforts in relation to the areas of knowledge and skill covered by the other workbooks in the series?
- Can I reflect objectively on my own thinking, feeling and willing?
- Can I recognize when I need to work on my core personal skills through personal development?

- You should be better able to see how your thinking can become more penetrating and creative

Nowadays everybody must think at work. Observation and concentration are necessary for sound thinking. There are some common biases in thinking that you need to watch out for. The ability to think about situations and things is a powerful technique for improving thinking. This leads to imagination, throwing off the usual constraints of thinking, and intuition, recognizing that

Reflect and review

we sometimes just 'know the answer' without apparent careful thought. We stressed that thinking needs practice and 'feeding' with new ideas and challenges. Questions here are:

- Can you think about your own thinking?
- Can you see ways your thinking could be improved?

■ You should be better able to recognize that feelings are an essential part of working life and that they can be assets not liabilities

Feelings are often neglected at work. They are an uncomfortable topic. But failing to take feelings into account leads to problems, especially in relations with others. Feelings can be suppressed until they burst out at an inappropriate time or place. Strong feelings, which may have their origins outside work or long in the past, can also intrude damagingly into working situations. A number of ways for managing feelings so that they remain appropriate and are neither suppressed nor intrusive were described. You explored the values that are important to you. Questions are:

- How aware are you of your feelings at work?
- Do your feelings make positive or negative contributions to your work?
- Could you usefully try out some of the ways for better managing feelings?
- Are you clear about the values you want to express at work?

■ You should be better able to work on your personal drive

Personal drive comes from wanting something strongly and having the inner resources, especially energy, to pursue it. Motivation can come from outer rewards, but commitment is stronger and longer lasting when rooted in personal values. Self-motivation can arise from an awareness of a gap between some aspect of how things currently are and how you would like them to be. Effectiveness is greatest when action is aimed at issues within your Circle of Influence. Ethical issues were briefly examined. When thinking, feeling and willing are congruent, effectiveness is likely to be high. Questions are:

- How strong is your personal drive?
- How could you increase your personal drive?
- Do you recognize ethical issues at work and can you manage them?

■ You should be better able to manage your learning and personal change to develop the capabilities you will need to stay effective

Personal development is about making yourself the object of a change programme. Development of yourself needs to be driven by a personal vision of how you would like to be. Fundamental principles of self-development are: accept responsibility, accept development takes time, be dedicated to reality, and keep a sense of balance. The learning underpinning development can be based on imitation, instruction (or better mentoring) or experience. Of these,

Reflect and review

experiential learning based on a conscious cycle of experience, review, learn and plan is often most effective for personal development. The need for support and to consider the needs of people close to you was discussed. Questions are:

- Do you accept the need for personal development?
- How can you work on your personal vision?
- Can you follow – some of the time at least – the principles?
- Can you find forms of learning and support that will facilitate your personal development?

2 Action plan

Use this plan to further develop for yourself a course of action you want to take. Make a note in the left-hand column of the issues or problems you want to tackle, and then decide what you intend to do, and make a note in Column 2.

The resources you need might include time, materials, information or money. You may need to negotiate for some of them, but they could be something easily acquired, like half an hour of somebody's time, or a chapter of a book. Put whatever you need in Column 3. No plan means anything without a timescale, so put a realistic target completion date in Column 4.

Finally, describe the outcome you want to achieve as a result of this plan, whether it is for your own benefit or advancement, or a more efficient way of doing things.

Desired outcomes					Actual outcomes
	1 Issues	2 Action	3 Resources	4 Target completion	

Reflect and review

3 Extensions

Extension 1 Book   *Lateral Thinking for Management*
              Author   Edward De Bono
              Edition   1990
              Publisher Penguin

De Bono is the originator of the term 'lateral thinking'. Any of the books by De Bono are worth reading. This one is especially aimed at managers, and gives plenty of techniques for improving the creative quality of your thinking.

Extension 2 Book   *Use Your Head*
              Author   Tony Buzan
              Edition   1995
              Publisher BBC

Again, like Edward De Bono, any of Tony Buzan's books are likely to be helpful in improving thinking. This one covers many techniques for reading, thinking, remembering, and so on. Tony Buzan has popularized the 'mind map' technique, and you will find an introduction to this here.

Extension 3 Book   *The Seven Habits of Highly Effective People*
              Author   Stephen R. Covey
              Edition   1992
              Publisher Simon & Schuster

This is a long book but well written and not difficult to read. Covey's approach is different to the one taken here, but entirely complementary. Do not expect to find easy techniques on how to be more effective. Covey draws a sharp distinction between what he calls the 'Personality Ethic' which aims to provide glib, superficial techniques (that might actually work – for a time) and the 'Character Ethic' which aims to develop deep personal qualities and skills.

Extension 4 Book   *Managing Yourself*
              Author   Mike Pedler and Tom Boydell
              Edition   1994
              Publisher Harper Collins

This contains many imaginative ideas and exercises. Like Covey's book and this workbook, Pedler and Boydell stress that effectiveness begins inside you and works from the inside to the outside.

Reflect and review

Extension 5

Book   *The Fifth Discipline*
Author   Peter M. Senge
Edition   1990
Publisher   Century Business

This is another important book. Its topic is the 'Learning Organization', and while it is all interesting and useful, Chapter 9, 'Personal Mastery', is the part most relevant to this workbook.

4 Answers to self-assessment questions

Self-assessment 1 on page 12

1. Being EFFICIENT is doing things right, being EFFECTIVE is doing the right things.

2. A manager needs to be effective at managing activities, RESOURCES, PEOPLE and INFORMATION.

3. Having the right knowledge and SKILLS is necessary but not sufficient for being effective.

4. Obstacles to effectiveness can be OUTER or INNER.

5. THINKING, FEELING and WILLING are core personal skills.

6. PERSONAL DEVELOPMENT is the process of improving your ability to manage yourself.

7. Examples of common outer obstacles to effectiveness are:
   - lack of time/opportunity to acquire new knowledge and skills
   - lack of time/opportunity to practise skills
   - lack of guidance or support from managers
   - lack of support from staff
   - lack of technical or human resources
   - lack of time
   - lack of information/poor communications.

8. The key person in improving your personal effectiveness is YOU.

Self-assessment 2 on page 28

1. Employees are no longer simply hands, nowadays everyone has to THINK.

2. The foundations of good thinking are OBSERVATION and CONCENTRATION.

3. If you want to picture how things could be, you must use your IMAGINATION.

Reflect and review

4   INTUITION is the faculty that gives us the answer, without having worked it out through logic and analysis.

5   Edward De Bono invented the term 'LATERAL thinking'.

6   People's FEELINGS are often overlooked or neglected at work.

7   The things in life that are important to us are our personal VALUES.

8   Examples of common biases in thinking:

- Selective attention
- Order effects
- Overconfidence in own experience
- Difficulty in changing one's mind
- Ease of availability
- Valuing according to source

9   Four ways of looking at a situation that are helpful in developing 'helicopter vision':

- Form
- State
- Function
- Purpose

10 The following are helpful in managing your feelings:

- Express your feelings in the moment
- Practise giving a feelings commentary
- Find a way to release feelings that you cannot express at work
- Feed your feeling life
- Take responsibility for your feeling life

Self-assessment 3 on page 46

1   Personal drive depends on how much you WANT something and how much ENERGY you have.

2   Motivation can arise from EXTERNAL REWARD but is better based on INNER VALUES.

3   Motivation to change something can arise from awareness of the gap between CURRENT REALITY and a potential IDEAL state of affairs.

4   Things we would like to do something about lie within our Circle of CONCERN but things we can actually affect lie within our Circle of INFLUENCE.

5   When what we think, feel and want are consistent with each other, then we can be described as CONGRUENT.

6   Our picture of how we would like to be is our personal VISION.

Reflect and review

7 The following are good principles for self-development:

- Accept responsibility
- Accept development takes time
- Be dedicated to reality
- Keep a sense of balance

8 The four phases of the experiential learning cycle are:

- Experience
- Review
- Learn
- Plan

5 Answers to the quick quiz

Answer 1 The four main areas where a manager must be effective are managing activities, managing resources, managing people and managing information.

Answer 2 Common 'outer obstacles' to effectiveness are:

- lack of time/opportunity to acquire new knowledge and skills
- lack of time/opportunity to practise skills
- lack of guidance or support from managers
- lack of support from staff
- lack of technical or human resources
- lack of time
- lack of information/poor communications.

Answer 3 'Inner obstacles' to effectiveness originate in ourselves.

Answer 4 Self-management means your ability to use your own personal resources in order to do your job effectively.

Answer 5 The four main areas to be managed in self-management are thinking, feeling, willing and personal development.

Answer 6 'Observation' can be defined as 'really seeing what is about you', and 'concentration' can be defined as 'staying with one topic long enough to develop a train of thought'.

Answer 7 Common biases in thinking include:

- Selective attention
- Order effects
- Overconfidence in own experience
- Difficulty in changing one's mind
- Ease of availability
- Valuing according to source

Reflect and review

Answer 8   To use imagination successfully you need to free yourself from past and current experiences and preconceptions, free yourself from linear thinking, and be willing to make jumps that have no logical justification.

Answer 9   Ways you can help manage your feelings include:

- Express your feelings in the moment
- Practise giving a feelings commentary
- Find a way to release feelings that you cannot express at work
- Feed your feeling life
- Take responsibility for your feeling life

Answer 10   Values work in everyday life by helping us choose where to direct our time and energy.

Answer 11   For strong personal drive you need to have a clear picture of what you want and enough energy to bring this picture into reality.

Answer 12   To be effective you should attend to things in your Circle of Influence.

Answer 13   Many ethical issues are not covered by laws, regulations or codes of conduct, but demand the exercise of personal values.

Answer 14   The four principles of personal development are:

- Accept responsibility
- Accept development takes time
- Be dedicated to reality
- Keep a sense of balance

Answer 15   The form of learning usually most suited to personal development is experiential learning.

Reflect and review

6 Certificate

Completion of this certificate by an authorized person shows that you have worked through all the parts of this workbook and satisfactorily completed the assessments. The certificate provides a record of what you have done that may be used for exemptions or as evidence of prior learning against other nationally certificated qualifications.

Pergamon Flexible Learning and NEBS Management are always keen to refine and improve their products. One of the key sources of information to help this process are people who have just used the product. If you have any information or views, good or bad, please pass these on.

NEBS MANAGEMENT DEVELOPMENT
SUPER SERIES
THIRD EDITION

Becoming More Effective

Dave Pearce

has satisfactorily completed this workbook

Name of signatory *Barbara Strudwick*

Position *Senior Training Consultant*

Signature *Barbara Strudwick*

Date *15 May 2003*

Official stamp
CORPORATE TRAINING & DEVELOPMENT
COUNTY HALL ANNEXE
COUNTY HALL
MARTINEAU LANE
NORWICH NR1 2UE

SUPER SERIES

SUPER SERIES 3
0-7506-3362-X   Full Set of Workbooks, User Guide and Support Guide

A. Managing Activities
0-7506-3295-X	1. Planning and Controlling Work
0-7506-3296-8	2. Understanding Quality
0-7506-3297-6	3. Achieving Quality
0-7506-3298-4	4. Caring for the Customer
0-7506-3299-2	5. Marketing and Selling
0-7506-3300-X	6. Managing a Safe Environment
0-7506-3301-8	7. Managing Lawfully - Health, Safety and Environment
0-7506-37064	8. Preventing Accidents
0-7506-3302-6	9. Leading Change
0-7506-4091-X	10. Auditing Quality

B. Managing Resources
0-7506-3303-4	1. Controlling Physical Resources
0-7506-3304-2	2. Improving Efficiency
0-7506-3305-0	3. Understanding Finance
0-7506-3306-9	4. Working with Budgets
0-7506-3307-7	5. Controlling Costs
0-7506-3308-5	6. Making a Financial Case
0-7506-4092-8	7. Managing Energy Efficiency

C. Managing People
0-7506-3309-3	1. How Organisations Work
0-7506-3310-7	2. Managing with Authority
0-7506-3311-5	3. Leading Your Team
0-7506-3312-3	4. Delegating Effectively
0-7506-3313-1	5. Working in Teams
0-7506-3314-X	6. Motivating People
0-7506-3315-8	7. Securing the Right People
0-7506-3316-6	8. Appraising Performance
0-7506-3317-4	9. Planning Training and Development
0-75063318-2	10. Delivering Training
0-7506-3320-4	11. Managing Lawfully - People and Employment
0-7506-3321-2	12. Commitment to Equality
0-7506-3322-0	13. Becoming More Effective
0-7506-3323-9	14. Managing Tough Times
0-7506-3324-7	15. Managing Time

D. Managing Information
0-7506-3325-5	1. Collecting Information
0-7506-3326-3	2. Storing and Retrieving Information
0-7506-3327-1	3. Information in Management
0-7506-3328-X	4. Communication in Management
0-7506-3329-8	5. Listening and Speaking
0-7506-3330-1	6. Communicating in Groups
0-7506-3331-X	7. Writing Effectively
0-7506-3332-8	8. Project and Report Writing
0-7506-3333-6	9. Making and Taking Decisions
0-7506-3334-4	10. Solving Problems

SUPER SERIES 3 USER GUIDE + SUPPORT GUIDE
0-7506-37056	1. User Guide
0-7506-37048	2. Support Guide

SUPER SERIES 3 CASSETTE TITLES
0-7506-3707-2	1. Complete Cassette Pack
0-7506-3711-0	2. Reaching Decisions
0-7506-3712-9	3. Making a Financial Case
0-7506-3710-2	4. Customers Count
0-7506-3709-9	5. Being the Best
0-7506-3708-0	6. Working Together

To Order - phone us direct for prices and availability details
(please quote ISBNs when ordering)
College orders: 01865 314333 • Account holders: 01865 314301
Individual purchases: 01865 314627 (please have credit card details ready)

We Need Your Views

We really need your views in order to make the Super Series 3 (SS3) an even better learning tool for you. Please take time out to complete and return this questionnaire to Management Marketing Department, Pergamon Flexible Learning, Linacre House, Jordan Hill, Oxford, OX2 8DP.

Name: ....

Address: ....

....

Title of workbook: ....

If applicable, please state which qualification you are studying for. If not, please describe what study you are undertaking, and with which organisation or college:

....

Please grade the following out of 10 (10 being extremely good, 0 being extremely poor):

Content	....	Appropriateness to your position	....
Readability	....	Qualification coverage	....

What did you particularly like about this workbook?

....
....
....

Are there any features you disliked about this workbook? Please identify them.

....
....
....

Are there any errors we have missed? If so, please state page number: ....

How are you using the material? For example, as an open learning course, as a reference resource, as a training resource etc.

....

How did you hear about Super Series 3?:

Word of mouth: ☐   Through my tutor/trainer: ☐   Mailshot: ☐

Other (please give details): ....
....

Many thanks for your help in returning this form.